THE DOWNFALL OF BEING REAL

Unspoken Commandments of Loyalty and Survival

BY

ROBERT AMPARAN

Introduction

Realness isn't just about being tough; it's about standing firm in your principles when the world pushes you to break. In a time where authenticity is rare, being real is more than just a label or a surface-level image—it's a way of life. Loyalty to self and others defines who you are. It's in your word, your actions, and your mindset, even when the world tries to mold you into something you're not.

But here's the thing about being real—it's not easy. In fact, it's a path that can be more isolating than rewarding. In a society that often glorifies betrayal, dishonesty, and shortcuts to success, staying true to your values can feel like a losing game. We're told that loyalty is a weakness, that principles hold us back, and that the only way to win is to compromise. Yet, for those who refuse to fold, the weight of being real can lead to downfall.

The downfall of being real comes when you realize that the same authenticity that defines you can be your undoing. People you thought were loyal vanish when times get tough, and those you trusted show their true colors when opportunity knocks. It's in these moments of betrayal and abandonment that being real is put to the test. It's easy to question why you continue to stand firm when the world seems intent on shaking your foundation.

This book is for those who feel the pressure to break but refuse. It's for the ones who stay loyal even when loyalty is a rarity, who hold onto their principles even when it would be easier to let go. Through these pages, we'll explore the cost of being real, the sacrifices it demands, and why—despite it all—it's still the only way worth living.

Because in a world full of fakes, being real may bring you to your knees, but it also keeps your soul intact.

Foreword by Lil Durk

Reading this book took me on a journey back to my own personal situations, making me reflect on the things I've been through and where I'm headed. With everything I've experienced, staying focused on growth has always been the mission. The commandments laid out in these pages hit different—they're principles I believe everyone should live by. They speak to survival, loyalty, and knowing how to move in a world where trust is rare. This isn't just a book; it's a guide. I recommend it to anyone trying to level up, stay grounded, and navigate life the right way.

The Cost of Loyalty

Loyalty comes with sacrifices, whether in business, friendships, or relationships. It's about giving without expecting, and in a world of betrayal, how do you keep that loyalty pure?

Table of Contents

Introduction 2

Foreword by Lil Durk 4

The Cost of Loyalty 5

Chapter 1 8

The Origins of Loyalty 8

Chapter 2 15

The Rules of Loyalty 15

Chapter 3 24

The High Price of Loyalty 24

Chapter 4 32

The Weight of Survival 32

Chapter 5 40

The Price of Silence 40

Chapter 6 53

Strangers Are Sometimes Better 53

Chapter 7 60

The Dangers of Being Too Accessible 60

Chapter 8 67

Play Broke and See 67

Chapter 9 74

Never Confuse Business with Brotherhood 74

Chapter 10 79

The Weight of Empty Promises 79
Chapter 11 85
Forgiveness: The Key to Moving Forward 85
Chapter 12 90
Redemption and Rebirth 90
Chapter 13 98
Reflections and Revisions 98
    Acknowledgments 104

Chapter 1

The Origins of Loyalty

Loyalty isn't something you're born with—it's something you learn, shaped by the world around you. And for me, that world wasn't soft. It wasn't a place where people hugged you after you fell or where they helped you back up when you were down. I grew up in a world that swallowed the weak, that took advantage of the kind. A world that fed you the idea that loyalty was a two-way street, but then turned around and left you stranded on the side of the road when you needed it the most.

I didn't learn about loyalty from some mentor, or from watching movies where the hero always wins. I learned loyalty through absence, through pain. I learned what it meant to stand by people when no one stood by me. And that's a lesson you can't teach in school. It's something life burns into your skin, deep enough that you never forget it.

"A Childhood of Absence"

When my mother passed away, I was too young to understand what death really meant. But I did understand what it meant to be alone. My father wasn't around—hell, he was like a ghost, someone people talked about but no one ever saw. I used to hear stories about him from my family. They'd tell me about how he was this larger-than-life figure, this Mexican man with a swagger and charm that could get him out of any situation. He was the kind of guy that, when he walked into a room, people noticed. But all I had were stories. He wasn't there to show me what that looked like. He wasn't there to teach me how to be a man, how to stand up for myself, how to survive.

So, from an early age, I had to teach myself.

I think part of me clung to those stories about my father because they gave me something to believe in. I was searching for an identity, trying to figure out who I was when the two people who made me weren't there. My mother was gone, and my father, well, he was never really there to begin with. I never knew my Hispanic side of the family the way I knew my mother's side, but there was always love—on my side, at least.

But love that isn't returned still leaves you empty, and I had to learn to fill that emptiness in other ways.

The streets taught me early that nobody owes you anything. Not love, not loyalty, not respect. You have to earn every ounce of it, and even when you do, there's no guarantee it'll come back to you. That's the first lesson the streets give you: Loyalty is rare, and most people don't know what to do with it.

"Proving Yourself When There's Nothing to Prove"

I spent most of my life trying to prove my loyalty to people who didn't deserve it. Maybe it was because I wanted the love I never got. Maybe it was because I thought if I gave enough, someone would finally see me the way I saw them. But it doesn't work like that.

When you're loyal, when you're real, people see that as weakness. They think you'll always be there, that no matter how many times they cross you, you'll still show up. And for a while, I did. I kept showing up for people who wouldn't cross the street for me. I kept giving to people who had nothing to give back but excuses and lies. I wanted to be the one they could rely on, the one they could trust, because in my heart, I thought that's what mattered. I thought that loyalty was something people would respect in the end.

But here's the harsh truth: Most people don't respect loyalty because they don't understand it.

They don't know what it feels like to give without expecting. They don't know what it means to stand by someone, even when it costs you something. They only know how to take. And that's what I had to learn the hard way—being loyal in a world full of takers makes you a target.

"Loyalty in the Streets"

The streets aren't like a family. They don't love you. They use you. The same streets that teach you to be tough are the ones that will leave you broken, bleeding, and alone. I saw it happen time and time again. Friends turning on each other, people smiling in your face while they were plotting behind your back. And through it all, I stayed real. I kept my word, even when it would've been easier to break it. I helped people who didn't deserve it, gave second chances to people who burned me the first time.

Why? Because I wasn't raised with a blueprint on how to be anything else. I learned from the absence, from the emptiness that surrounded me. I didn't have someone to tell me that loyalty could be a dangerous thing, that it could get you killed just as easily as it could get you respect. And respect, that's what I wanted. More than love, more than money—I wanted people to look at me and know I was real. I wanted to be remembered as someone who stayed true, even when the world tried to break me.

"When Loyalty Hurts"

But loyalty hurts. It's not some badge of honor that you wear, and people pat you on the back for. It's a scar that keeps bleeding, and the more you give, the deeper it cuts. I've been crossed over by people I thought were my brothers. I've been hurt by women I thought I loved. I've been finessed in business deals that were supposed to be about trust and partnership.

Each time it happened, I felt the sting of betrayal, but I didn't let it turn me bitter. Instead, I kept it moving. That's another lesson I learned: Loyalty isn't about holding grudges—it's about knowing when to let go and move forward.

People will hurt you, they'll cross you, and they'll make you question why you ever gave them your loyalty in the first place. But if you let that turn you into someone you're not, they've won. They've broken you. And I swore a long time ago, I would never let anyone break me. I might bend, but I won't break.

"Loyalty is a Test"

Loyalty is tested when the odds are against you, when the easy thing to do would be to walk away or turn your back. But I never took the easy route. I've walked through fire for people who wouldn't even get their shoes wet for me, and yeah, it hurts. But I wear those scars with pride because, at the end of the day, I stayed true to who I was.

That's the real cost of loyalty—you give and give, and sometimes, all you get in return is pain. But it's that pain that shapes you, that molds you into someone who understands that loyalty isn't about what you get back. It's about knowing who you are, even when the world tries to make you forget.

Loyalty is standing firm when everything around you is falling apart. It's being there, even when no one else is. It's staying real, even when life gives you every reason to be fake.

And that's where it all began for me—in a world that took everything from me, I gave back loyalty. Even when it wasn't deserved. Even when it wasn't returned.

Because that's who I am.

Chapter 2

The Rules of Loyalty

Loyalty is not a game. It's not something you pick up when it's convenient or set down when it becomes uncomfortable. Loyalty is a code, an unspoken set of rules that governs your every move, even when the world tells you it's okay to break them. The thing about loyalty is that it's not just about being loyal to other people—it's about being loyal to yourself, to your own principles, to your own word.

The streets will try to bend you, to make you forget who you are. They'll throw situations at you where breaking your own rules seems like the smart move, the easy move. But that's the test. Because loyalty isn't tested when things are easy—it's tested when things are falling apart, when the pressure is on, when your back is against the wall. And most people fail that test.

"The Unspoken Commandments of Loyalty"

Nobody hands you a book on loyalty when you're growing up. Nobody sits you down and says, "This is how you live your life by the code." You learn by watching, by experiencing, by getting burned and sometimes burning others in the process. Loyalty doesn't come with a user manual—it's something you feel deep inside, a sense of right and wrong that you can't explain but you know is real.

But over time, I developed my own commandments, rules that I lived by even when it cost me. These rules weren't taught in school, and they weren't written down. They were forged in the streets, in late-night conversations with people I trusted and long nights spent thinking about where I went wrong.

1. Never Outshine the Master

The first commandment I ever learned about loyalty came from one of the most powerful books I ever read: The 48 Laws of Power. Law number one, Never outshine the master, has stuck with me throughout every phase of my life. It's not about bowing down to anyone or being a follower—it's about knowing when to step back and let others take the spotlight. It's about respecting the power dynamics in any relationship or situation.

The streets are full of people who are constantly looking over their shoulder, paranoid that someone's coming to take their spot. And the truth is, most of them are. But when you're loyal to someone, when you've made a commitment to stand by them, you don't cross that line. You don't try to one-up them, don't try to make them feel like they need to compete with you. Instead, you play your role.

That's what people don't understand—there's strength in knowing your role. There's wisdom in understanding that sometimes the best way to rise is by letting someone else think they're on top. It's about knowing that your loyalty to them doesn't mean you have to dim your light forever—it just means you wait for your moment. Because your time will come.

2. Stay True to Your Word

In a world where people lie for sport, keeping your word is rare. And that's exactly why it's valuable. Your word is the one thing nobody can take from you, but once you give it away and break it, you've lost it forever. People don't forget when you fail them, and they don't forgive it easily.

I learned early on that people would lie to your face and not think twice about it. They'll tell you they've got your back, that they'll never switch up, that they'll ride with you till the wheels fall off. But when push comes to shove, when life gets hard, most people will save themselves first. They'll throw you under the bus without a second thought if it means saving their own skin.

But me? I always kept my word, even when it hurt me. I knew that my reputation, my name, was all I had in this world. If I told you I'd be there, I showed up. If I said I'd handle something, I handled it, no excuses. And that's what set me apart from most people. Because when you move like that, people notice. Even the ones who can't stand you will respect you.

But keeping your word isn't just about business deals or promises you make to other people—it's about the promises you make to yourself. When you tell yourself that you're going to stay true, that you're going to move with integrity, you can't break that promise just because it's easier to lie or cheat. You have to live by that, even when no one's watching.

3. Endure in Silence

One of the hardest lessons I learned was how to suffer in silence. I don't mean that you should bottle up your pain until it breaks you, but there's a strength in knowing when to keep your struggles to yourself. The streets don't care about your pain. They don't care if you're tired, if you're broken, if you're running on empty. People might ask you how you're doing, but most of the time, they don't really want to know. They just want to see if you're weak enough for them to take advantage of.

So I learned to endure in silence. When I was hurting, when I was betrayed, when I was down bad, I kept it to myself. I didn't broadcast my pain because that's when people swoop in to kick you while you're down. I handled it internally, I dealt with it in the quiet moments when nobody was around. And when I came back, I came back stronger. People never knew how close I was to breaking, because I never gave them the satisfaction of seeing me vulnerable.

There's a certain power in silence. People expect you to react, to break down, to lose your cool when life hits you hard. But when you hold it in, when you deal with it on your own terms, you take control of the situation. You let the pain fuel you, but you don't let it consume you. And that's where real strength lies—not in pretending you're invincible, but in knowing how to endure when life tries to break you.

4. Respect Given, Respect Earned

The streets run on respect, but respect isn't given freely. It's earned, and once you lose it, it's almost impossible to get it back. Respect isn't about fear, though—people get that confused. It's not about making people scared of you or forcing them to acknowledge your power. It's about how you carry yourself, how you move in silence, how you keep your word.

I learned early that respect has to go both ways. If I respected you, I expected the same in return. But here's the thing—most people will take your respect and never give it back. They think that just because you respect them, they can walk all over you. And that's when you have to draw the line.

There were times when I gave people respect they hadn't earned yet, thinking it would come back to me. But respect doesn't work like that. You can't give it to everyone. Some people will take your respect as a sign of weakness, thinking they can manipulate you or take advantage of your kindness. That's when I had to learn to pull back, to be more selective about who I showed respect to.

But when someone did earn my respect, they had it for life. I would go to war for those people. Because in a world where most people are out for themselves, having someone who respects you on a deep level is rare. And when you find that, you protect it.

5. Stay Down Until You Come Up

This is more than just a motto to me—it's a way of life. Staying down means sticking to your principles when the world tries to shake you. It means grinding through the hard times without complaining, knowing that your time will come if you stay true. Too many people give up when they're just inches away from the breakthrough. They lose faith, they start doubting themselves, and they fold under pressure. But me? I've always stayed down, because I know that nothing worth having comes easy.

Life threw everything at me—betrayal, heartbreak, failure—but I didn't let it break me. I stayed humble, stayed grinding, even when nobody was watching, even when it felt like the world had forgotten about me. That's the thing about loyalty—it's not just about being loyal to other people; it's about being loyal to yourself, to your own goals, to your own dreams. You can't give up on yourself just because life gets hard.

Staying down means weathering the storm. It means understanding that success isn't an overnight thing—it's a long, painful process that tests every part of who you are. But the reward isn't just in the success; it's in knowing that you didn't compromise your principles to get there. You didn't betray yourself to win.

"The Lonely Road of Loyalty"

The thing about loyalty is that it's a lonely road. Most people don't live by the same code, and that makes you an outsider. You'll lose friends. You'll lose relationships. You'll walk away from business deals that could've made you rich because you refuse to compromise your integrity. And that's okay. Because at the end of the day, all you have is your word and your principles.

Loyalty demands sacrifice. It demands that you give up the easy path, the shortcuts, the temptation to betray others for your own gain. And that's why most people aren't loyal. They can't handle the weight of it. They want the rewards without the struggle. But the truth is, the real reward is knowing that you stayed true to who you are.

Chapter 3

The High Price of Loyalty

Loyalty is expensive. It costs you more than most people are willing to pay, and if you're not careful, it'll take everything you have. People romanticize the idea of being loyal, but they don't talk about what it really costs—the sleepless nights, the lost opportunities, the heartbreak, and the constant feeling that you're giving more than you're getting. It's not a pretty story. It's raw. It's painful. And it's real.

The truth is, loyalty will drain you. It'll test every ounce of strength you have, push you to your breaking point, and leave you questioning everything. You'll wonder if it's worth it, if being real is worth all the pain that comes with it. But here's the catch: once you're committed to being loyal, there's no turning back. There's no halfway. You're either all in, or you're just like the rest—willing to betray at the first sign of discomfort.

"Loyalty Will Break You First"

Before loyalty rewards you, it'll break you. That's the part nobody talks about. Everyone wants to talk about loyalty as if it's this beautiful, noble thing that people admire. But to get to that point, you have to go through the fire. Loyalty will put you in situations that test the very core of who you are. It'll make you question your own judgment, make you wonder if it's even worth it to stay down for people who would never do the same for you.

There was a time when I believed in the good in people. I thought that if I was loyal enough, if I showed people that I had their back no matter what, they would return the favor. I thought loyalty was contagious, that if you were real, it would inspire others to be real too. But the truth is, loyalty doesn't work like that. Loyalty is a one-sided contract most of the time. You give, and give, and give, and people will take.

And that's the part that breaks you—realizing that most people aren't built the way you are. They don't live by the same code, they don't value the same things, and they damn sure don't have the same loyalty you do. You'll be out here giving people the world, and they won't even notice. They'll take your kindness as a weakness, your loyalty as an opportunity to use you, and when they're done, they'll leave you behind without a second thought.

"The Pain of Betrayal"

There's no pain like betrayal. It cuts deeper than any physical wound, and the worst part is, it almost always comes from someone you trust. Someone you let in. Someone you thought had the same code as you. But that's the harsh reality of loyalty—betrayal is always lurking around the corner. It's the price you pay for putting your faith in people, for believing that they'll be as real as you are.

I've been crossed over more times than I can count. Friends I considered family turned their backs on me when things got tough. People I broke bread with, people I went to war for, switched up when they saw an opportunity to benefit themselves. And every time, it felt like a knife to the heart. But what hurt the most wasn't the act of betrayal itself—it was the fact that I never saw it coming.

When you're real, when you live by a code, you assume other people will do the same. You expect that if you've been loyal to someone, they'll be loyal to you. But most people don't think like that. Their loyalty is conditional, based on what they can get from you. And the moment you stop being useful to them, they cut ties.

The thing about betrayal is, it changes you. It makes you colder. It makes you second-guess everyone and everything. But the real test is whether or not it breaks you. Because loyalty demands that you keep going, even after you've been stabbed in the back. It demands that you don't let the betrayal of others turn you into someone you're not.

"The Loneliness of Loyalty"

The further you go down the road of loyalty, the lonelier it gets. That's the reality most people don't talk about. Being loyal means standing on your own more often than not. It means watching people drift away because they're not willing to walk the same path. It means losing friends, distancing yourself from family, and cutting ties with people you thought would be there for life.

When you live by a code, it isolates you. You see the world differently. You move differently. And most people don't understand that. They can't comprehend why you're so strict about principles, why you're willing to sacrifice relationships for the sake of staying real. They think you're stubborn, that you're too rigid. But the truth is, it's not about stubbornness—it's about survival. You've seen what happens when you compromise your values, when you betray your own sense of right and wrong. You've seen how quickly things can spiral out of control when you stop being real.

Loyalty is lonely because most people aren't built for it. They want the benefits of loyalty, but they don't want to deal with the consequences. They don't want to endure the sacrifices, the pain, the isolation. So they bail. They switch up. They move on to something easier, something that doesn't require as much effort.

And that leaves you standing there, alone. But that's the price. You have to be okay with walking this path by yourself sometimes. You have to understand that loyalty isn't about having a crowd around you—it's about staying true to yourself, even when nobody else is around.

"The Mental Strain"

What people don't understand is how much of a mental toll loyalty takes on you. It's exhausting. Constantly being the one who holds everything together, who stands firm when everyone else is falling apart, who's always there for people, wears you down. It's draining to always be the strong one, to always be the reliable one, even when you're falling apart inside.

Loyalty isn't just a physical burden—it's mental. It's waking up every day and choosing to stay real, even when you don't feel like it. It's knowing that people are going to let you down and still choosing to be there for them. It's staying true to your word, even when breaking it would make your life so much easier.

The mental strain of loyalty is something that most people will never understand. They'll never know what it feels like to be pulled in a hundred different directions, to have people depending on you when you can barely stand on your own two feet. They don't know what it's like to carry the weight of other people's problems because you promised you would.

It messes with your head. You start to question yourself, start to wonder if you're being stupid for holding on to this code that nobody else seems to live by. You wonder if it's worth it, if staying real is worth the price you're paying. But deep down, you know the answer. Because even when the mental strain is breaking you, the alternative—being fake, being disloyal, compromising your principles—feels even worse.

"The Temptation to Switch Up"

There will be times when the temptation to switch up is almost unbearable. When you're tired of being the one who's always real, always loyal, always standing by your word. When you're tired of being the one who's always hurt because you're the one who cares. In those moments, it's easy to think about changing. About becoming like everyone else—selfish, cold, calculating.

But that's where loyalty is truly tested. Because anyone can be loyal when things are good, when the road is smooth. The real test comes when you're tired, when you're drained, when you're hurt. That's when loyalty shows its true colors. And that's when most people fail.

The temptation to switch up is real, and I've felt it more times than I'd like to admit. There were moments when I thought about giving up, when I thought about turning my back on people the same way they had turned their backs on me. But every time, I came back to the same conclusion—being fake would break me in ways that betrayal never could.

Being fake would mean betraying myself, and that's a price I wasn't willing to pay.

"Loyalty as a Lifeline"

Loyalty isn't just something I gave to others—it was something I held onto for myself. It was my lifeline, the thing that kept me grounded when everything else was falling apart. When the streets were cold, when life was harsh, when I had nobody else, my loyalty to myself kept me moving. It was the one thing that couldn't be taken from me, the one thing I controlled.

There's a kind of peace in knowing that no matter what happens, no matter how many people switch up, no matter how many times you get betrayed, your loyalty is yours. It belongs to you. And that's a power most people don't understand. They think power is in money, in status, in control. But real power is in loyalty—because loyalty can't be bought, and it can't be stolen.

Chapter 4

The Weight of Survival

Survival isn't just about staying alive. It's about learning how to live with everything that tries to kill you—whether that's betrayal, poverty, or your own mind. Survival is an art. It's a skill that requires toughness, strategy, and the ability to endure more than most people can handle. It's about taking hit after hit and still standing up, even when every part of you is telling you to stay down.

The hardest part about survival isn't the fight—it's the aftermath. It's learning how to live with the scars, the memories, and the knowledge that nothing and no one is truly safe. Once you've been through enough, you start to see the world differently. You start to understand that survival isn't just about getting through the day—it's about carrying the weight of everything you've lost along the way.

"The Heavy Hand of Life"

Life has a way of hitting harder than any punch. It doesn't matter how strong you think you are, how prepared you try to be—life will humble you. It'll take everything you thought you knew and twist it, leaving you standing there with nothing but questions. And the worst part is, life doesn't care if you're ready for the hit. It doesn't care if you're in a good place or a bad place. It strikes when you least expect it.

I learned that the hard way. I spent years thinking I could outsmart the world, that if I was tough enough, if I worked hard enough, I could avoid the pain. But that's not how life works. Pain is inevitable. No matter who you are or where you come from, life will hit you where it hurts the most. And the thing about pain is, you can't predict it. You can't control it. All you can do is survive it.

I remember the day I realized that life doesn't owe anyone anything. I was young, still thinking that if I played my cards right, I could avoid the worst of it. But life doesn't play by the rules. It doesn't care if you've been good, if you've been loyal, if you've done everything you were supposed to do. It'll take everything from you in the blink of an eye and leave you to pick up the pieces on your own.

"The Battle Inside"

Survival isn't just a physical struggle—it's a mental war. And that war is constant. You can't run from it. You can't hide from it. It's with you every second of every day. It's the voice in your head that tells you to give up, that whispers you're not strong enough, that you don't have what it takes to keep going.

The hardest battles I've ever fought weren't with other people—they were with myself. There were times when I felt like the world was too heavy, like I couldn't take another step. Times when the darkness inside felt too strong, when the weight of everything I'd been through felt like it was suffocating me.

And the truth is, I almost gave in. I almost let the darkness win. Because survival is exhausting. It's draining. It's waking up every day and knowing that you have to fight—again. Even when you don't want to. Even when you're tired. Especially when you're tired.

But that's the thing about survival—it's not about winning every battle. It's about refusing to lose the war. It's about making the choice, day after day, to keep going. To keep fighting, even when it feels like you have nothing left.

"The Loneliness of the Strong"

Being strong comes with a price. The stronger you are, the more people lean on you, and the more you realize how few people are willing to lean back. When you're the one who's always holding it together, people start to think you don't need help. They start to think you can carry it all on your own. And maybe you can—but that doesn't mean you should have to.

The thing about being strong is that it isolates you. People respect strength, they admire it, but they don't understand it. They don't see the cracks forming beneath the surface, the weight that's slowly breaking you down. They don't see the nights when you lie awake, wondering if you're ever going to feel whole again. All they see is the exterior—the part of you that's still standing, still fighting.

I've learned that strength is a lonely road. The more you show people that you can handle, the more they expect you to handle. They don't offer help because they assume you don't need it. And after a while, you stop expecting it. You stop looking for someone to have your back, because you've been disappointed too many times.

But the truth is, everyone needs someone. No matter how strong you are, no matter how tough, there's a limit to what you can carry alone. And when you've spent your whole life being the strong one, it's hard to admit that you need help. It's hard to admit that sometimes, the weight is too much. But that's part of survival too—learning when to let go, learning when to ask for help, even when it feels like weakness.

"The Burden of Loss"

Survival is also about loss. It's about learning how to live with the things you can never get back. People talk about survival like it's this heroic thing, like it's all about overcoming obstacles and coming out on top. But they don't talk about the losses that come with it. They don't talk about the people you lose along the way, the parts of yourself that get left behind.

Loss is a constant companion when you're trying to survive. You lose people, you lose dreams, you lose parts of yourself that you never thought you'd have to let go of. And the hardest part is, you can't dwell on it. You can't sit in your grief, because the world doesn't stop for you to heal. You have to keep moving, keep pushing forward, even when it feels like everything is falling apart around you.

I've lost more than I ever thought I could handle. I've lost family, I've lost friends, I've lost parts of myself that I'll never get back. And every loss chips away at you, takes something from you that you can never replace. But that's part of survival too—learning how to keep going, even when you've lost everything that mattered.

The weight of loss doesn't get lighter. You just get stronger. You learn how to carry it, how to live with it, how to make room for the pain without letting it consume you. But it's always there, in the background, a reminder of what you've been through and what you can never get back.

"Resilience in the Face of Failure"

Failure is a part of survival. It's not a question of if you'll fail, but when. And when it happens, it'll knock the wind out of you. It'll make you question everything you thought you knew about yourself. But the key to survival isn't avoiding failure—it's learning how to get back up after it knocks you down.

I've failed more times than I can count. I've made mistakes, I've trusted the wrong people, I've put my faith in things that were never meant to last. And every time, it felt like the end. It felt like the world was collapsing around me, like I was never going to recover. But here's the thing about failure—it's not final. It feels like it is, but it's not.

Failure is a teacher, if you let it be. It'll show you things about yourself that you never knew. It'll reveal your weaknesses, your blind spots, the areas of your life that need work. But it'll also show you your strength. It'll show you that you're capable of surviving things you never thought you could.

Resilience isn't about avoiding failure—it's about learning how to bounce back from it. It's about understanding that every failure is just a stepping stone on the path to survival. It's about refusing to let failure define you, refusing to let it break you.

"The Unseen Battle"

Survival is full of battles that nobody else sees. It's the quiet struggle, the fight you face alone, the moments when you're on the edge and nobody else knows. These are the moments that define you—the ones where nobody is watching, where there's no applause, no recognition, just you and the choice to keep going or to give up.

People think survival is all about the big moments—the life-or-death decisions, the major turning points. But the truth is, survival is built in the small moments. It's in the decision to get out of bed when you don't feel like it. It's in the choice to keep working when you're exhausted. It's in the moments when you feel like giving up but decide to keep fighting anyway.

These unseen battles are the hardest ones. They're the ones that take the most out of you, because they're the ones you fight alone. But they're also the ones that build the most strength. Because when you win those battles, when you make it through those dark moments, you prove to yourself that you're stronger than the world gives you credit for.

Chapter 5

The Price of Silence

Silence is heavy. It carries more weight than any words ever could, and it has the power to shape a life in ways you can't see until it's too late. Silence is both a weapon and a shield, and most people spend their lives trying to find a balance between the two. But the truth is, silence has a cost, and that cost isn't always visible on the surface. Sometimes, it buries itself deep inside you, growing like a sickness until it's all you know.

"The Quiet Burden"

People think strength is loud. They think it's about being vocal, about showing the world that you're tough. But real strength—true strength—often comes in silence. It's the ability to carry your pain quietly, to bear the weight of your struggles without needing to shout about them. It's the decision to face the world without letting it see the cracks beneath the surface.

But that kind of strength comes with a price. Carrying your pain in silence can be suffocating. It eats away at you, little by little, until you don't even recognize yourself anymore. And the longer you stay silent, the heavier the burden becomes. You learn to live with the weight, but it changes you. It hardens you. It makes you cold in ways you never intended.

I learned early on that silence was my only option. In a world where nobody wanted to hear your pain, where people turned their backs on you the moment you showed weakness, silence was survival. Speaking out—asking for help—felt like an invitation to be broken down, to be judged. So, I swallowed my pain and carried it alone.

But silence has a way of isolating you. It pushes you into your own head, makes you feel like you're on an island surrounded by people who could never understand. And after a while, you stop trying to reach out. You stop expecting anyone to see the weight you're carrying. And that's when the silence becomes dangerous—when it becomes more than just a way to protect yourself. It becomes a prison.

"The Dangers of Holding It In"

There's a difference between being strong and bottling everything up. For a long time, I thought they were the same thing. I thought that if I didn't talk about my pain, if I kept it buried deep enough, it would eventually disappear. But that's not how it works. The pain doesn't go away—it just festers. It builds and builds until it has no choice but to explode, and by then, the damage is done.

When you hold everything in, when you refuse to let anyone see what's going on inside, you're setting yourself up for disaster. You become like a ticking time bomb, waiting for the smallest trigger to set you off. And when that moment comes, it's not just the pain that comes out—it's everything. Every hurt, every betrayal, every disappointment you've ever faced comes crashing down, and it's overwhelming.

I've been there. I've felt the explosion—the moment when years of bottled-up pain came rushing to the surface and left me gasping for air. And the worst part is, nobody saw it coming. Because I'd been so good at keeping it all inside, at pretending that everything was fine. But the truth was, I was drowning. I was suffocating under the weight of my own silence, and by the time I realized it, it was too late to stop the flood.

"The Fear of Vulnerability"

Silence is often rooted in fear—fear of vulnerability, fear of rejection, fear of being seen for who you really are. It's easier to stay quiet than to risk opening up and being judged. It's easier to pretend that everything's okay than to admit that you're struggling, that you're hurting, that you need help.

Vulnerability is terrifying. It requires you to strip away the armor you've spent years building, to expose the parts of yourself that you've worked so hard to hide. And for people like me, who've been hurt too many times to count, that's not something we do lightly. Because we know that vulnerability can be a weapon in the wrong hands. We know that once you open up, you give people the power to hurt you in ways you never imagined.

So, we stay silent. We build walls around ourselves, walls that keep the pain in but also keep the world out. And over time, those walls become harder and harder to break down. We convince ourselves that we don't need anyone, that we're better off alone. But the truth is, silence is a lonely place. It may protect you from the world, but it also keeps you trapped in your own pain, with no way out.

"The Unspoken Pain of Others"

One of the hardest lessons I've learned is that everyone is carrying their own silent pain. Just because someone seems like they've got it all together, just because they don't talk about their struggles, doesn't mean they're not fighting their own battles. Silence doesn't mean someone is fine—it often means the opposite.

I used to think that I was the only one who carried my pain in silence. I thought that everyone else had it easier, that they didn't have the same struggles. But as I got older, I started to see the cracks in other people's facades. I started to notice the way their eyes flickered when they thought nobody was watching, the way they hesitated when asked how they were doing.

People are good at hiding their pain. They're good at pretending that everything is okay, because the world has taught them that showing vulnerability is a weakness. But if you look closely, you'll see the signs. You'll see the way they carry themselves, the way they keep a certain distance, the way they laugh a little too loudly or stay silent a little too long.

We're all carrying something.

"The Cold Reality of Betrayal"

Betrayal cuts deeper than any wound. It's not the kind of pain you can see, but it's the kind that leaves scars all over your soul. It changes you in ways you never expected—makes you hard where you used to be soft, makes you cautious where you used to trust. It doesn't matter how tough you are, how strong you've made yourself, or how careful you try to be—betrayal finds its way in. And when it does, it tears you apart from the inside out.

The truth about betrayal is that it never comes from your enemies. It's always from the people you trusted, the ones you let close enough to hurt you. That's what makes it burn so deep. You expect the world to be hard, you expect strangers to be unkind, but betrayal—real betrayal—comes from those you never thought would turn on you.

"The Slow Poison of Trust"

Trust is dangerous. It's the most fragile thing in the world, and yet we give it away, sometimes without thinking. And when that trust is broken, it doesn't just hurt—it shatters everything. You begin to question everything, from your own instincts to the people who still stand by you. Was your judgment flawed from the start? Did you miss the signs? Were you naive, or just too hopeful in a world that's never lived up to those hopes?

I've learned the hard way that trust isn't just about faith in others—it's also about faith in yourself. When someone betrays you, it shakes your confidence in your own ability to see the truth. You wonder if you were ever good at reading people at all. It makes you doubt everything, and that doubt lingers long after the betrayal itself has faded.

Betrayal makes you paranoid. It makes you look over your shoulder constantly, even when there's no reason to. You start expecting everyone to let you down, because if the ones closest to you could do it, what's stopping anyone else? It's like a poison that seeps into everything. You think you've moved on, but it's always there, lurking in the back of your mind, reminding you that no one is truly safe.

"The Cost of Guarding Your Heart"

Once you've been betrayed, you start building walls. Not just to keep others out, but to protect whatever is left of yourself. You can't afford to let anyone in too deep, not anymore. The price of trust is too high. The walls you build aren't just physical—they're emotional, mental. You close off parts of yourself, the vulnerable parts, because you can't risk letting someone get close enough to hurt you again.

But here's the thing about walls—they keep everyone out, even the people who might deserve to be let in. You start to confuse safety with isolation. The walls protect you, but they also trap you. They keep the pain at bay, but they also keep out the possibility of real connection, of real healing. And after a while, you forget how to let those walls down.

I've spent years behind those walls. I've convinced myself it's better this way, that it's safer to rely on no one but myself. But the truth is, it's lonely. When you don't let anyone in, you also don't let anyone help carry the load. You bear everything alone, and it's heavy. Heavier than anyone should have to carry. But the alternative—letting someone in and risking betrayal again—is even more terrifying.

"The Lessons of Pain"

Pain is a teacher. It's a brutal, unrelenting teacher, but it's effective. Betrayal teaches you things you would never have learned otherwise. It forces you to confront parts of yourself that you'd rather ignore. It shows you your own weaknesses, your blind spots, your vulnerabilities. And while those lessons come at a cost, they also make you stronger, if you let them.

One of the hardest lessons I've learned is that not everyone has the same heart as you. You can be loyal, you can be genuine, you can be everything you promised to be—and people will still betray you. Not because of who you are, but because of who they are. Betrayal isn't a reflection of your worth; it's a reflection of their character.

I've had to learn not to take betrayal personally, even though it feels personal. It feels like a direct attack on everything you are, but it's really not about you. It's about the person who chose to betray you. It's about their greed, their fear, their selfishness. That doesn't make it hurt any less, but it helps you understand that it's not your fault. You can't control other people's actions, no matter how much you wish you could.

"Rebuilding After the Fall"

The hardest part of betrayal isn't the pain itself—it's figuring out how to move forward. Once the trust is broken, once the damage is done, how do you rebuild? How do you look at the world with the same eyes, knowing what you know now? The answer is—you don't. You can't go back to who you were before. Betrayal changes you, whether you want it to or not.

But that doesn't mean you can't rebuild. It just means you have to do it differently. You have to learn how to protect yourself without closing yourself off completely. You have to learn how to trust again, but this time with caution, with wisdom. You don't give your heart away so freely, but you also don't let the fear of betrayal rule your life.

Rebuilding after betrayal is slow. It's painful. There's no roadmap for how to do it, no clear path to follow. You have to take it day by day, step by step. Some days, you'll feel like you're making progress, like you're finally moving forward. Other days, the weight of it all will come crashing back down, and it'll feel like you're right back where you started. But that's part of the process. Healing isn't linear—it's messy, it's complicated, and it takes time.

"The Power of Letting Go"

One of the most difficult lessons I've had to learn is the power of letting go. When someone betrays you, the natural reaction is to hold on to the pain, to let it fuel your anger, your sense of injustice. But holding on to that pain only hurts you. It doesn't fix anything, it doesn't change what happened, and it doesn't make the betrayal any less real. All it does is keep you stuck in the past, reliving the hurt over and over again.

Letting go isn't about forgiveness. It's not about excusing what happened or pretending it didn't hurt. It's about choosing not to let the betrayal define you. It's about freeing yourself from the grip that pain has on your life. It's about reclaiming your power, your sense of self, and deciding that the betrayal doesn't get to dictate your future.

Letting go is hard. It's one of the hardest things you'll ever do, because it feels like you're giving up something that's rightfully yours—the anger, the hurt, the sense of being wronged. But in reality, holding on to that only keeps you trapped. It doesn't serve you, it only weighs you down.

"The Quiet Strength of Moving On"

There's a quiet strength in moving on from betrayal. It's not the loud, triumphant kind of strength that people talk about. It's not the kind that gets applause or recognition. It's the kind of strength that shows up in the everyday moments, in the decision to keep living your life, even after everything's fallen apart.

Moving on doesn't mean you forget what happened. It doesn't mean the betrayal stops hurting. But it means you refuse to let it control you. It means you choose to live your life in spite of the pain, in spite of the betrayal. And that takes more strength than most people realize.

There's a kind of peace that comes with moving on. It's not the absence of pain, but the acceptance of it. It's the understanding that betrayal is a part of life, that people will hurt you, and that you can't stop it. But you can control how you respond to it. You can choose to rise above it, to keep going, to rebuild and become stronger in the process.

"The Wisdom of Experience"

Betrayal brings with it a kind of wisdom that only experience can teach. It shows you the truth about people, about the world, and about yourself. It strips away the illusions, the naivety, and forces you to confront the reality of human nature. But it also gives you a clarity that few other experiences can. It shows you who you can trust, who you can't, and most importantly, it shows you that you are stronger than you ever thought you could be.

The wisdom that comes from betrayal is hard-earned. It doesn't come quickly, and it doesn't come easily. But once you have it, it stays with you. It becomes a part of who you are, shaping the way you see the world, the way you move through life.

This wisdom teaches you that betrayal is inevitable, but it's not the end. It's just one chapter in a much larger story. And while it may change you, it doesn't have to break you. You learn to expect less from people, but you also learn to give more to yourself. You learn that survival isn't about avoiding pain—it's about enduring it, learning from it, and coming out the other side stronger.

Chapter 6

Strangers Are Sometimes Better

There's something strange about how loyalty works. You spend years with people, build history with them, share experiences, laugh, cry, fight, and somehow, they start slipping. You think that because you've known someone for 20 years, they'll be the first to support you, the ones to hold you down without question. But what I've come to realize is that time doesn't mean shit when it comes to loyalty. In fact, the ones you've known the longest are often the ones who let you down the hardest.

I was just talking with my homie Cade about this the other day. He was saying the same thing I've been feeling for a long time—how it seems like your 20-year homies are worse than the new ones. I felt that in my soul. It's not that time erases loyalty, but it's like people get too comfortable with who you are, who you've been to them, and they stop putting in the effort. They start thinking that just because they've been around, they're automatically loyal. But loyalty isn't something you get from just being in someone's life. It's something you have to keep earning, keep proving, no matter how long you've known someone.

People get lazy with their loyalty. They start assuming that because you're homies, they don't have to show up anymore. They take you for granted, think you're always going to be there, no matter what. But that's not how it works. I don't want to have to beg for support. I need it to be real, to be genuine. If it's not, then those people have no business being around me.

It's like when Cade and I were talking—he said something that hit me hard: "Sometimes you gotta disappear for people to understand your value." And that's real. You stick around too long, people start treating you like you're just part of the scenery. They get used to you being there, so they don't feel the need to support you like they should. But the second you disappear, the second you stop showing up for them, they start realizing what they had.

I've had to do that—disappear. Not because I wanted to, but because I had to remind people what loyalty looks like. You shouldn't have to explain loyalty to the ones closest to you, but somehow, they're the ones who need the lesson the most. It's crazy how someone you've known for years will act like you're asking for too much just because you expect the same loyalty you've been giving.

And then you meet new people—strangers, really. People who have no history with you, no long-standing connection, and they show more support in a few months than your so-called day ones have shown in years. It's a wild reality to face, but it's true. It's not the time you've spent together that matters—it's the respect they have for who you are right now.

New people see you for who you are in this moment, not who you were. And because of that, they can recognize your value quicker. They're not bogged down by old memories, by comfort, by the idea that they don't need to support you because they've already "earned" their place in your life. New people are hungry—they want to prove their loyalty because they see something in you that your old friends have forgotten.

When I think about it, it's almost like loyalty has an expiration date for some people. They think that once they've been loyal for a certain amount of time, they don't have to keep proving it. But that's not how loyalty works. Loyalty is like a muscle—

you have to keep working it, keep strengthening it, or it'll atrophy and die. Just because we've been cool for years doesn't mean you get a free pass to stop showing up for me.

I had to learn this the hard way. Growing up on the west side of Chicago, loyalty wasn't just something we talked about—it was survival. If someone had your back, you could make it through anything. But I also learned that the ones you expect to ride for you are often the ones who switch up when you need them most. You don't see it coming because you've built this idea in your head that time equals loyalty. You assume that the longer someone's been in your life, the stronger their loyalty is. But it doesn't always work like that.

Sometimes, the person you met last week will show you more loyalty than the one you've known for decades. And that's because they're not jaded by the past—they're in the moment, and they're showing up for you because they believe in who you are now. They don't have all that history clouding their judgment. They see you as you are, not as you were.

It's easy to get comfortable when you've been around someone for years. It's easy to think that because you've got history, that's enough. But loyalty is about more than just time—it's about actions. I don't care if we've been cool since we were kids. If you're not supporting me now, if you're not riding for me when it counts, then that history doesn't mean shit. You've got to return the loyalty you expect. It's a two-way street, and too many people forget that.

You know what's crazy? It's not even about asking for loyalty. You shouldn't have to ask. Loyalty should be given freely, without expectation, without conditions. When you're loyal to someone, you don't need to be reminded. You just show up because that's what loyalty is—showing up even when it's inconvenient, even when it's hard, even when you don't feel like it.

But too many people only want to be loyal when it benefits them. They want to ride for you when things are good, but the second shit gets tough, they're nowhere to be found. And that's the difference between old homies and new ones sometimes. The new ones don't have any preconceived notions about who you are. They're not stuck in the past, thinking about the times you fell off or the mistakes you made. They see you for the person you are now, and they respect that.

That's why strangers can sometimes be stronger. They don't have the baggage that comes with years of friendship. They're not weighed down by comfort or entitlement. They're just there, supporting you, because they see something real in you. And in return, you've got to be loyal to them, too. It's not about testing people, but you can't keep giving loyalty to those who don't deserve it. You've got to be smart about who you let into your circle.

That's something I've been learning more and more as I get older. Loyalty isn't something you can just expect from people because of time. You've got to choose your crowd wisely. If people aren't supporting you, if they're not showing up for you, then they're not your people. And you've got to be willing to let them go, no matter how long they've been in your life.

You can't beg for loyalty. You can't beg for support. If it's not real, it's not worth your energy. And trust me, there are people out there who will show up for you without you even having to ask. They might be strangers now, but they'll be stronger than the ones you thought were loyal. That's just how it is. And once you realize that, you start moving different. You stop chasing loyalty from people who don't value you and start building with the ones who do.

It's a hard lesson, but it's necessary. You can't keep giving yourself to people who aren't giving back. Loyalty is a two-way street, and if the ones you've known for years aren't holding up their end, it's time to stop carrying the weight for them. Sometimes, the new people in your life, the ones who show up unexpectedly, are the ones who will hold you down the hardest. And that's the kind of loyalty that matters—the kind that's proven through actions, not just words.

Chapter 7

The Dangers of Being Too Accessible

There's a hidden danger in being too accessible. The more you're seen, the more people think they understand you. They start believing they know your every move, your patterns, your weaknesses. In this game of life, especially when you've got something to lose, being too accessible can be your downfall. You open yourself up to the "back door" — that setup from people you thought had your back. It's a hard truth, but even those who swear they're loyal can be wolves in sheep's clothing. And the worst part? You won't see it coming if you're too caught up in being seen, in being present for everyone all the time.

I try to teach this to my brother Coka. He's not just my homie—he's family. And family, we protect each other, not just physically but mentally. I tell him all the time, "Don't let people feel like they know everything about you. Keep something back, something for yourself." When people think they know your every move, they start getting comfortable.

And when they're comfortable, that's when they think they can backdoor you.

See, it's a strange thing. We're not God—we don't know who's who. People say they're loyal, but how can you really know? You can't. Not fully, anyway. That's why you've got to watch everyone, even the ones who claim to ride for you. People's intentions shift. Money, jealousy, power—it all changes the way people look at you. They may have started out solid, but over time, that loyalty erodes, and if you're too accessible, you'll miss the signs. You'll be too busy being around, being in their face, to notice that their vibe has shifted. That their eyes don't hold the same respect anymore.

That's why I believe in mastering the art of disappearing. Not ghosting, no. You've still got to be in their face, but only when it benefits you. When you become a ghost, it's not about cutting everyone off or hiding—it's about control. Control of how much of you people get to see, and control over your energy. Too much access? That breeds comfort, and when people get comfortable, they forget who you are. They forget that you're not someone to be played with.

There's power in being seen and then gone. Let them miss you. Let them wonder what you're up to, because the minute they think they've got you figured out, you're vulnerable. And in these streets, vulnerability is a weakness that can cost you your life. I've seen it happen too many times. Someone starts getting too comfortable, letting people too close, and before they know it, they're on the wrong end of the setup, wondering how the ones they thought were loyal ended up being their downfall.

You've got to understand—there's always someone watching. Always someone looking for an opening. And that's why you have to play your cards close. You can be friendly, you can be cool, but don't let them feel like they know everything about you. There's a difference between being accessible and being available. Accessible means people can reach you anytime, anywhere, but being available means you control when they get access. It's about boundaries. Knowing when to step back, when to remove yourself from situations before they turn deadly.

Coka, my brother, he's got a big heart. He's loyal to the bone, but I always remind him—loyalty doesn't mean you owe everyone your presence. You've got to protect yourself first.

And it's not about paranoia; it's about survival. You don't know who's who, not really. People will smile in your face, share a drink with you, but be plotting on your downfall the entire time. If you're too accessible, you give them the playbook to take you out.

And I've been in situations where I realized too late that being too accessible was setting me up for failure. You start thinking people are cool just because you've been around them for years, because they've been down with you for so long. But that's the biggest mistake. Time doesn't equal loyalty, and accessibility doesn't guarantee trust. Just because someone's been in your life for years doesn't mean they deserve all of you. It doesn't mean they're not capable of being the ones to backdoor you when you least expect it.

You've got to be smart. Know when to be seen, and more importantly, know when to disappear. You don't need to be at every event, at every gathering. Sometimes, you've got to fall back, let people wonder what you're up to. Let them think twice about where you stand because that uncertainty? That's your power. If they can't predict your moves, they can't plot against you. If they don't know where you are or what you're doing, they can't set the trap.

It's a balance—being close enough to stay connected but distant enough to keep them guessing. And yeah, people might start talking, saying you've switched up, that you've gone ghost, but let them talk. Let them wonder. You don't owe anyone an explanation for how you move. And anyone who feels entitled to your time, your presence, isn't someone you need around anyway.

I try to live by this, and I try to instill it in my people, especially Coka. He's got a big future ahead of him, but only if he learns to protect himself in the right way. You can be loyal without being accessible. You can be solid without being present for everyone all the time. And if they're really for you, if they're really loyal, they'll understand that. They'll respect your distance because they know it's not personal—it's survival.

People think loyalty means being available 24/7, but that's a lie. Real loyalty means understanding when to step back and let the other person breathe. It means giving space, not demanding it. The ones who demand your presence all the time, who get mad when you don't answer their calls or show up to every function, those are the ones you need to watch.

Because real friends, real family, they understand the value of moving in silence.

Look, in this world, you've got to watch everyone. And I don't say that to make you paranoid, but you can't be naive. You've got to pay attention because slipping up just once could cost you everything. The backdoor is real, and it's always unlocked if you're too accessible. People are always looking for a way in, a way to get close enough to take advantage of you. And sometimes, it's the ones who've been around the longest who are the most dangerous. They know your patterns, your weaknesses, and if you're not careful, they'll use that against you.

I tell Coka this all the time—keep them guessing. Don't let people feel like they've got you figured out. Move in ways they can't predict. Disappear when you need to, but show up when it's least expected. Let them think they know you, but always keep a part of yourself hidden. That's how you survive. That's how you make sure no one ever gets close enough to backdoor you.

You can't stop people from plotting, but you can make sure they never get the chance to follow through. And that starts with not being too accessible. Control your energy, control your presence, and control the narrative. Let them see what you want them to see, but never let them feel like they know the whole story. Because the minute they think they know you, that's when you become vulnerable. And vulnerability in this game? It can cost you your life.

Chapter 8

Play Broke and See

There's a strange power in playing broke. When you strip away the flash, the cars, the image people have of you, and reveal nothing but the bare bones of your situation, you see people for who they really are. That's when the truth comes out. No one can hide behind their own desires or their expectations of you anymore. Playing broke isn't just about testing loyalty—it's about being loyal to yourself. It's about stepping back from the façade and looking around, seeing who stays when they think you've got nothing to give.

When I signed with Lil Durk, everything changed—or at least it seemed like it did. I was on tour, driving luxury cars, staying in the finest mansions. Everywhere I went, people wanted a piece of me, like I had made it to the top. Everyone thought I was rich. But let me tell you something: I was broke. It's wild to say that, but it's true. I was riding high on the wave of fame and success, but behind the scenes, I was struggling in ways no one could imagine. I had it all in front of me, yet I had nothing.

Yeah, it was fun. The crowds, the energy, the feeling of being on top. But the truth was I was fucked up, and it wasn't a secret to me. People didn't care about what I really had, though. They saw me standing next to Durk and automatically thought I was the savior, like I had pockets deep enough to fix everyone else's problems. It was like I had a neon sign above my head that said, "This man can save you." And I tried. I really tried. There were times I went broke just to impress people who didn't have shit themselves. The thought of it now makes me laugh, but at the time, I was trying to live up to expectations that weren't even mine.

It's crazy how people can project their own needs onto you. They saw me living a certain way and thought I had everything they wanted. People didn't ask if I was good, if I was straight—they just assumed. And I wanted so bad to meet that image, to be the man they thought I was. I started going out of my way to live that lifestyle, not for myself, but to keep up appearances for others. And that's when it hit me—the game is completely fucked up.

The real twist? It wasn't just the people around me; it was me. I wanted to look rich more than I actually wanted to be rich. That's a hard truth to swallow, but it's real. I was chasing an image, trying to live up to the hype, when in reality, I wasn't focused on building anything real for myself. I was fronting, plain and simple. And after a while, it got old. The luxury cars, the mansions, the designer clothes—they all felt empty. I realized I was impressing people who didn't even have anything, and that wasn't doing anything for me but dragging me further into the hole.

That's when I started to take a step back and think about my future. I started investing—my money, my time, my energy—into things that would last. I had to shift my mindset. It wasn't just about looking like I had it anymore; it was about actually having it. I realized I needed to make moves that would set me up for the long run, not just for the moment.

But along the way, I learned one of the most valuable lessons—sometimes you've got to play broke to see who's real. Not because you need people to prove themselves, but because when you strip away the surface, you start to see what people are really about. You'll find out quickly who's around for the wrong reasons when they think you've got nothing to offer them. If they're still standing by you when the money's gone, when the lifestyle isn't glitz and glam anymore, that's when you know who's truly down for you.

I used to test people like that. Play broke, act like I didn't have it, and watch how they moved. You'd be surprised how many faces change when they think you can't give them what they want. They start fading away, distancing themselves, or even worse, they start pressing you harder, trying to squeeze what they can out of you before it's too late. And that's when you've got to make a decision—are you going to keep entertaining those people, or are you going to let them show themselves the door?

Never let people know exactly what you have. That's a rule I live by now. Everybody's got different reasons for being around, and some of those reasons aren't as pure as you might think. People are out for themselves, and that's just the way it is. When you're up, they're all in your face, showing love, acting like they're down for the ride. But the moment they think you're not in a position to do anything for them, they're gone, or worse—they're plotting. You see, people want to attach themselves to success, not struggle. They're not interested in helping you build; they just want to be there when the house is already standing.

I had to learn that the hard way. You want to believe people are with you for the right reasons, but the truth is, not everyone is. I used to think that loyalty was something you could feel, something you could just sense in someone. But loyalty, real loyalty, is only proven when there's nothing left to gain. And that's where playing broke comes in. When people think you've got nothing, you'll find out real quick who's still down for you and who was just around for what they could get.

That's why I don't show all my cards anymore. I had to start playing the game differently. Keep things to myself, move smarter, and most importantly, stop trying to impress people. It's a waste of time and energy, and in the end, the only person you're letting down is yourself. I had to stop caring about how people saw me and start caring about how I saw myself. That's when I started to make real progress.

Playing broke showed me the truth about people, but it also showed me something about myself. I had to get comfortable with the fact that not everyone's going to stick around when they think you've got nothing to offer. And that's okay. Let them leave. Let them walk away. You don't need people like that in your circle anyway. The real ones, they'll stay, even when the chips are down. They'll ride with you through the struggle because they see your potential, not just what you can do for them in the moment.

And it's funny, because when you start moving like that, when you stop showing off and just focus on building, the right people start to come into your life. You attract what you project. When you're trying too hard to look like something you're not, you attract the wrong crowd. But when you're real, when you're focused on growing, that's when the real ones come around.

I remember being on tour, trying to keep up with the lifestyle, and realizing I was running in circles. I wasn't investing in myself; I was investing in an image. But once I shifted that, everything changed. I stopped worrying about what people thought and started worrying about my own future. And in that process, I realized something else—it's not just about playing broke to see who's real; it's about playing broke to remind yourself of what's real.

When you're broke, you have to be resourceful. You have to think about every move you make. You can't afford to waste time or money on things that don't matter. That's when you start seeing life clearly, without all the distractions. And when you come back from that, when you start building again, you do it with a different mindset. You stop chasing after people's approval and start chasing after your own goals. You learn to separate the ones who are with you for the right reasons from those who are just waiting to see what they can get out of you.

That's a lesson I try to pass on to anyone who's trying to come up. Don't worry about impressing people. Don't spend your last trying to keep up with an image that's not real. Invest in yourself, and let the chips fall where they may. Play broke, and see who's really down. See who sticks around when the money's gone, when the shine fades, and all that's left is you. That's where the real loyalty lies.

Chapter 9

Never Confuse Business with Brotherhood

Loyalty runs deep, but when it comes to mixing personal relationships with business, the line can get blurry. I learned that the hard way with JP, a friend I had grown to love over time. JP was cool, no doubt. He was the kind of friend you'd have a good laugh with, ride out with, and he'd be down for whatever. But when the stakes got higher, when it came time for me to really level up, I started seeing things in him that I couldn't ignore. There was always something that held him back, like he wasn't ready to make the changes that came with growth. And when I signed with Durk, all of that became clear.

When I got with OTF, it wasn't just about music; it was about aligning with something bigger. The streets already know the politics. I was a GD—a Gangster Disciple—by affiliation, but OTF was all BD—Black Disciple. And trust me, them OTF niggas were BD crazy! Now, don't get it twisted, that wasn't the issue with JP. I didn't change up because of the difference in affiliations. I knew how to move between those lines because, at the end of the day, it wasn't about gang ties; it was about growing beyond that. I was focused on making moves, on securing the bag, and staying out of the drama. But JP? He didn't get that.

JP was stuck in that mindset. He was the kind of dude who couldn't see past the block, the beefs, or the street politics. Always running his mouth, ready to argue, ready to fight. And in the environment we were in, that could get you killed, fast. It wasn't that I didn't love him—I did—but I couldn't afford to have someone around me who was reckless. I had to start thinking bigger, thinking long term. Every decision I made wasn't just about me; it was about my future, my family, and my survival. JP wasn't ready to make that shift.

When I signed with Durk, JP felt like I changed, like I had switched up on him. He thought it was about me being around all BDs now, like I had left him behind because of the affiliation. But that wasn't it. It wasn't about OTF versus the GDs. It was about growth versus stagnation. I saw it coming, though. JP wasn't trying to grow. Every time we were together, it was the same old drama—arguing over petty shit, getting into fights, acting wild. And the more I tried to move forward, the more I realized he was pulling me back. I couldn't let that happen, not when I had everything on the line.

At a certain point, I had to make a choice: do I keep holding onto this friendship and risk everything I'm building, or do I fall back for the sake of my own progress? That's when I learned one of the most important lessons in my life: never confuse business with brotherhood. Just because someone's been your friend doesn't mean they're meant to be a part of your business journey. And when business is involved, things can get real tricky, real fast.

JP took my distance personally, but it wasn't about that. It was about survival. You can't afford to mix personal feelings with business decisions. The moment you do, you risk losing everything. I had to fall back, and it hurt because JP was my dawg. But I'd rather fall back and protect both of us than let things escalate into something that couldn't be undone. That's the thing about loyalty—sometimes the most loyal thing you can do is walk away before things get worse.

I live by a code: I'd rather cut you off than let things get to a point where we can't come back from it. I'd rather walk away than hurt my brother. Loyalty isn't about sticking around for the dysfunction; it's about knowing when to let go for the sake of peace. Business is business, and the bros are the bros. You can't mix the two. When you get older, you start to realize that no one's gonna pay your bills for you. No one's going to put food on your table. So, while loyalty is essential, it's not an excuse to let personal feelings cloud your judgment. You have to take care of your business first and foremost.

It's hard, though. When you're in the middle of it, you think loyalty means sticking together no matter what. But loyalty also means knowing when to pull back, knowing when to protect yourself. You can't expect people to grow just because you are. And sometimes, those you think will ride with you forever just aren't built for the road you're on. It doesn't mean they're bad people, but they're not the right people for your journey.

I tried to teach JP that, but he wasn't trying to hear it. He was too caught up in what he thought loyalty meant. He didn't understand that in business, feelings can't run the show. There's no money in your feelings—just heartaches. That's when I started to distance myself, to focus on my own moves.

I knew it would be a lonely road at times, but that's the price of success.

Chapter 10

The Weight of Empty Promises

Promises have a weight to them. They carry the expectation of something real, something solid, a bond that holds two people together across time and space. When those promises are broken, that weight doesn't just disappear—it shifts, settling deep into your soul like a stone. And for some of us, those broken promises start early. They teach us that even the people closest to you, the ones you're supposed to rely on, can be the first to let you down.

I'll never forget the day my stepfather left me on my aunt Dorothy's porch. He looked me in the eyes and said, "I'll be back, don't worry." I was just a kid, probably too young to understand the full scope of what was happening, but old enough to know what a promise was. I clung to his words like they were the only thing keeping me from falling into a pit I couldn't climb out of. He drove away that day, and I sat on the porch waiting. For how long? I couldn't tell you. Hours turned into dusk, dusk turned into night, and I was still sitting there.

Eventually, Aunt Dorothy brought me inside, but the cold realization that he wasn't coming back had already set in. That was how I started out on the west side of Chicago—alone, abandoned, and with a promise that evaporated into thin air.

You learn a lot about the world from moments like that. I learned early that promises were fragile things. People threw them around like they meant something, but too often they didn't. My stepfather's promise was the first one I remember being broken, but it damn sure wasn't the last. It felt like after that day, everyone around me thought it was open season to finesse Hypno. Like I had a sign on my back that said, "Promise him the world, then walk away."

Promises stopped meaning anything real. People would look me in the eye, swear on their own lives, and still disappoint me. You start seeing patterns after a while. The ones who smile the most, talk the most, swear up and down that they're different, are usually the first to let you down. It's like they think words are enough. That just because they said something, it became true. But I know better. Words are empty unless backed by action. And I've had enough broken promises in my life to know when someone's lying before the words even leave their mouth.

I wasn't just disappointed—I was angry. Angry that people thought they could just walk away without any consequences. That they could lie to my face and act like it didn't matter. It made me hard in ways I didn't even understand at the time. I stopped expecting people to come through for me. Stopped trusting that anyone would ever really show up when it mattered. When you're young, you're supposed to believe in the people around you. You're supposed to trust that when they say they're going to do something, they mean it. But I didn't get that. I got the cold truth. And that truth was: nobody cares as much as you do. Not your stepfather, not the friends you thought you could rely on, not the people who said they had your back. Nobody.

That's the kind of lesson that stays with you. It builds walls around your heart. By the time I hit my teenage years, I was already a master at spotting the fakes. I could see through people's lies before they even had the chance to speak them. But what I didn't realize was that being able to see through it didn't stop the weight from piling up. Each broken promise was like another brick added to the load I was carrying. And over time, that weight became unbearable.

Every time someone let me down, it reinforced that deep-seated belief that nobody was ever going to be real with me. They'd all just keep trying to finesse me, just like they'd done since I was a kid. I thought I was being smart by not letting anyone get close, but the truth was, I was just scared. Scared that if I let myself believe in people again, I'd end up back on that porch, waiting for someone who was never coming.

It's painful when you realize that the people you once trusted are the same ones who betray you. When your stepfather looks you in the eyes and lies, it's like a crack forms in your foundation. And over time, more lies create more cracks until everything starts falling apart. The weight of all those broken promises becomes too much to bear.

People talk about loyalty like it's this sacred thing, but loyalty means nothing if it's not backed by action. My stepfather promised he'd be back, and he never showed. Friends would tell me they'd hold me down, and they'd disappear when things got tough. Over and over, I saw the same story play out, and after a while, I stopped expecting anything different. Loyalty wasn't something you found—it was something you gave, and people either returned it or they didn't. But more often than not, they didn't.

On the west side of Chicago, where I grew up, people were always hustling. Always looking for an angle, for a way to get one over on you. Loyalty? It was just another word in the streets. Everybody claimed to have it, but few ever actually did. I remember how it felt when I realized the game wasn't fair, that no matter how real you kept it, there would always be people trying to finesse you. It didn't matter if they knew you for years or just a few months. People were always looking out for themselves first, and any promise they made was just a convenient way to keep you around until they didn't need you anymore.

It's a cold truth, one that I learned young. Promises don't mean shit unless they're backed by actions. And most people? They ain't about action. They're about talking, about making themselves look good in the moment, about saying what they think you want to hear. But when the time comes to follow through, they're nowhere to be found. Just like my stepfather, they're gone, leaving you alone with the weight of another broken promise on your shoulders.

You start to wonder if anyone is really capable of keeping their word. If there's anyone out there who isn't just looking to finesse you the same way everyone else has. And that's where the real pain comes in—because deep down, you still want to believe. You want to believe that there's someone out there who will stand by their word, someone who will show up when they say they will. But every broken promise makes that hope a little harder to hold on to.

The weight of empty promises doesn't just sit on your chest—it seeps into your bones. It changes the way you look at the world, at people. It makes you question everyone's intentions, makes you wonder if anyone is truly real. And the more it happens, the more you start to believe that maybe it's just you. Maybe you're the one who keeps expecting too much. Maybe you're the one who's too loyal, too real for the world around you.

But the truth is, it's not you. It's the people who think promises are just words, the ones who think loyalty is optional. They're the ones who are broken, not you. And once you realize that, you stop waiting for them to change. You stop waiting on promises that were never real in the first place.

Chapter 11

Forgiveness: The Key to Moving Forward

Forgiveness was a lesson I learned through pain, betrayal, and ultimately growth. It's easy to hold onto anger and resentment, especially when someone close to you betrays your trust. I've spent countless hours, days, and even years trapped in a cycle of negativity because I couldn't let go. I look back and realize I wasted so much time complaining about one person and their actions that I lost sight of my own progress. It became a habit—a toxic routine that held me prisoner while they lived their life without a second thought. I was the one who ended up suffering.

The moment I made the conscious decision to forgive, a heavy weight lifted off my shoulders. I started to understand that forgiveness isn't about excusing the actions of those who wronged you; it's about liberating yourself from the chains of resentment. It was only then that I realized how deeply intertwined forgiveness is with self-care and personal growth.

There was a particular moment that stands out, a painful reminder of how the streets don't play fair. Someone I considered family—a brother in every sense of the word—backstabbed me for money. Not just a few dollars, but half a million. That's a lot of cash, and instead of us building something great together, he had other plans. I won't dive into the exact details; sometimes, the specifics are too raw to recount. But what I will say is this: betrayal by someone you trust cuts deeper than any knife.

This was a person I had taken in as family, someone who swore loyalty to me. Yet in the end, that loyalty proved to be nothing more than a façade. It was a harsh wake-up call. It showed me that just because someone says they love you or claims to be with you, it doesn't mean they have your best interests at heart. Actions speak louder than words, and it took me too long to learn that lesson.

I had to come to terms with the fact that the streets are merciless. They'll chew you up and spit you out if you let them. When you dwell on betrayal, it creates a poison in your mind. You find yourself going over the same thoughts, the same anger, and you're just left feeling more lost and broken.

I realized I didn't want to spend another year clinging to this grudge, so I made a choice to forgive, to let go of that weight.

Forgiveness doesn't mean I'm forgetting what happened. I still remember the sting, the sense of betrayal, but I've learned to live with it. What I like to say is, "I forgive, but I never forget." It's a motto that has served me well. It reminds me that while I won't let the past define me, I will use it as a lesson. It's a way of acknowledging that while people make mistakes—some of which they may never come back from—I have the power to move on.

There were times when I allowed my pride to get in the way, times when I thought holding onto the pain made me stronger. But in truth, it only made me weaker. Life is too short to be carrying around that kind of baggage. Holding onto anger for too long isn't just harmful; it's exhausting. I had to put my pride aside and accept that forgiveness doesn't mean weakness. It's a sign of growth, maturity, and understanding.

Trust me; it's going to be okay. When you forgive, you're not just freeing the other person; you're freeing yourself. You're creating space for better things to come into your life. The moment I chose to forgive that betrayal was the moment I started to heal. I began to focus on my goals and aspirations instead of wallowing in past pain. I shifted my energy to where it mattered, to the things that would propel me forward rather than keep me stuck in the past.

This chapter is essential because I want my audience to understand that forgiveness is a gift we give ourselves. It's not about absolving the other person; it's about reclaiming your peace. The streets will always be tough, and not everyone is going to have your back. But you don't have to let that define your journey. Learn to forgive, even when it's hard. People make mistakes—some grievous—but that doesn't mean you have to dwell on them.

Forgiveness is an act of love, not just for others but for yourself. You're allowed to move on, to live your life without being shackled by the weight of resentment. It's okay to put your pride down for a moment and embrace the reality that life is too short for grudges. When you make that choice, you open up a world of possibilities.

So, to anyone reading this: when you find yourself in a situation where you feel betrayed or hurt, take a step back. Evaluate how much energy you're investing in that negative emotion. Is it worth it? I can assure you, the answer is no. Let it go. Give yourself the gift of forgiveness. It will not only lighten your spirit but also pave the way for better relationships, opportunities, and experiences.

Life is about moving forward, and forgiveness is the key that unlocks that door. You'll feel a sense of relief that you didn't think was possible. Trust me; I've been there. I forgave, I moved on, and now I can see the world through a clearer lens. Don't dwell on the past; learn from it and use that knowledge to build a better future. It's not just about living; it's about thriving.

Chapter 12

Redemption and Rebirth

The air is thick with the weight of silence, a silence that echoes the aftermath of all that has transpired. It hangs in the room like a heavy fog, suffocating yet oddly comforting, as if every broken piece has found its place in this desolate landscape. The past is a cruel teacher, but it can also be a catalyst for profound change, if only you allow it. To understand redemption, one must first traverse the dark, twisted paths of regret, pain, and confrontation with the self

"Confronting the Shadows"

Redemption begins not with the world outside but with the world within. It requires an honest confrontation with one's shadows—the parts of yourself you'd rather hide. For too long, I had been running from my past, from the pain that clung to my heels like a relentless ghost. I had learned to smile through the hurt, to wear my scars like badges of honor, but beneath that façade was a turmoil that demanded acknowledgment. I had to peel back the layers of denial, to look squarely at the anger, the guilt, and the sorrow that festered beneath the surface.

This journey into the self is neither easy nor linear. It is a winding road filled with pitfalls, a treacherous path where each step forces you to confront the truth of who you are. It means facing the choices you made, understanding the motivations behind those choices, and coming to terms with the consequences they wrought. Each revelation is a sharp blade, cutting through the skin of pretense and exposing the raw, pulsing truth beneath.

I sat in the dim light of my room, surrounded by the relics of my past—photos of lost friendships, remnants of broken promises. Each item was a reminder, a silent accusation, whispering tales of lost opportunities and shattered trust. I felt the tears sting my eyes, not from weakness, but from the strength of acknowledgment. To cry was to reclaim a part of myself that had long been silenced.

"The Burden of Regret"

Regret is a heavy burden, one that often weighs more than the original sin. It has a way of twisting your perception, turning the past into a kaleidoscope of 'what ifs.' What if I had made different choices? What if I had seen the signs? What if I had trusted my instincts instead of allowing fear to guide me? These questions echoed in my mind like a relentless drumbeat, each one driving deeper the nails of self-recrimination.

In the quiet moments of reflection, I began to understand that regret, while painful, is also an opportunity for growth. It offers a chance to learn from the past, to analyze the missteps that led to pain, and to extract wisdom from the wreckage. I started to write down my thoughts, to articulate the swirling chaos in my mind. The act of writing became a catharsis, a way to untangle the knots of regret that had tightened around my heart.

I crafted a letter to my former self, filled with both compassion and critique. I told her it was okay to make mistakes, to stumble along the path of life. I reminded her that the mistakes were not the end; they were the beginning of something new, an opportunity for redemption. Through that letter, I learned that forgiving oneself is the first step toward redemption, a prerequisite for moving forward.

"Forgiveness: The Key to Liberation"

Forgiveness is often painted as a noble act, but it is rarely easy. It is a multifaceted gem, reflecting different hues of understanding and acceptance. It begins with oneself—an act of self-compassion that acknowledges the humanity in our imperfections. I had to forgive myself for the choices I made, for the trust I misplaced, and for the hurt I had both experienced and inflicted. This was not about absolution; it was about liberation.

Once I began to forgive myself, I found that forgiveness extended to others became more attainable. The faces of those who had betrayed me danced before my mind's eye, their actions replaying like an unwanted film reel. I had built my walls high, fortified by anger and resentment, but I knew I had to dismantle them if I was ever to find peace. Each time I recalled a moment of betrayal, I fought to replace the bitterness with understanding.

Why had they done what they did? What void were they trying to fill? I realized that many betrayals stem from deep-seated insecurities, a reflection of the betrayer's own pain and inadequacies. As I acknowledged this truth, the shackles of resentment began to loosen. Forgiveness became a bridge—not a sign of weakness, but a testament to my strength.

"Finding Purpose in Pain"

Through the ashes of betrayal and regret, I began to glimpse a flicker of purpose. Pain has a way of redirecting our paths, forcing us to reassess what truly matters. I sought to transform my suffering into something meaningful, a way to reach out to others who were navigating similar storms.

I began volunteering at a local shelter, connecting with those who had faced their own betrayals and losses. Each story shared, each tear shed, reminded me of the common thread of humanity we all share. In the faces of others, I saw reflections of my own pain, but I also saw resilience.

There is a unique power in vulnerability; it creates bonds that can heal wounds. In sharing our stories, we create a collective strength that helps us to rise from the rubble of our past. I found that giving back allowed me to channel my pain into a purpose, transforming my scars into tools of empathy and understanding.

"The Beauty of Rebirth"

In time, I began to feel the stirrings of rebirth within me. It was as if the chrysalis of my old self was cracking open, revealing a new identity forged in the fires of experience. I started to embrace the complexities of my journey—the pain, the betrayals, the moments of doubt—and I recognized them as integral pieces of my mosaic.

Rebirth is not instantaneous; it is a gradual unfolding, much like the blooming of a flower after a long, harsh winter. Each day, I took small steps toward a brighter future. I learned to embrace vulnerability, to let others in, and to seek connection without fear of betrayal. I realized that to love fully means to risk heartbreak, but the potential for joy far outweighed the fear of pain.

As I moved forward, I began to cultivate practices that nourished my spirit—meditation, journaling, and moments of stillness where I could reflect on my journey. I found solace in nature, in the simple act of watching the sun set, reminding me that endings can be beautiful too.

"Embracing the Journey Ahead"

With each passing day, I grew more confident in my ability to navigate the complexities of life. I learned to view challenges as opportunities for growth, knowing that each struggle brought with it the potential for transformation. I had weathered storms that felt insurmountable, yet I emerged stronger and more resilient.

The journey toward redemption is ongoing; it is not a destination but a path that stretches before me, winding through valleys and peaks alike. I learned to embrace uncertainty, knowing that life is an ever-changing tapestry woven with threads of joy and sorrow. Each moment holds the possibility for change, for renewal, and for deeper understanding.

As I look back on the road I've traveled, I carry with me the lessons learned from betrayal, the wisdom extracted from regret, and the power found in forgiveness. I stand not as a victim of my circumstances, but as a survivor, a testament to the strength of the human spirit.

"The Final Reflection"

In the end, redemption is not about erasing the past or forgetting the pain. It is about integrating those experiences into the tapestry of who we are. It is about recognizing that we are all flawed, all searching for meaning, and all capable of growth.

The past may have shaped me, but it does not define me. I am more than my betrayals; I am a seeker of truth, a champion of healing, and an advocate for compassion. I carry forward the lessons learned and the strength gained, embracing the beautiful chaos that is life.

And as I step into the unknown future, I do so with an open heart and a resilient spirit, ready to embrace whatever comes next—fully aware that within every ending lies the potential for a new beginning.

Chapter 13

Reflections and Revisions

In the tapestry of life, each thread weaves a story marked by choices, relationships, and experiences. For many, the journey of self-discovery is continuous, punctuated by moments of reflection that compel us to reassess our paths. This chapter invites you to embark on an introspective journey—a chance to revisit the narratives of your life, reassess your commitments, and draft revisions that align with your authentic self.

"The Importance of Reflection"

Reflection is not merely a pause; it is an essential practice that allows us to extract meaning from our experiences. Psychologists assert that reflection promotes deeper learning and understanding. In a world that often prioritizes speed and productivity, taking the time to reflect can seem counterintuitive. Yet, it is in these quiet moments that we gain clarity about our values, aspirations, and the loyalties we hold dear.

Consider how often we move from one experience to the next without truly processing the lessons learned. We accumulate successes and failures, yet many of us fail to pause and analyze how these moments shape our identities. Reflection serves as a mirror, revealing both our strengths and areas for growth. This practice cultivates self-awareness and provides the foundation for meaningful revisions in our lives.

"Revisiting Core Values"

As we engage in reflection, we must ask ourselves: What are my core values? Our values serve as the compass guiding our decisions and actions. They are often forged in the crucible of life experiences—shaped by our upbringing, relationships, and the challenges we've faced. To identify these values, consider the following questions:

What principles do I stand by? Reflect on situations where you felt proud or fulfilled. What values were at play in those moments?

What experiences have challenged my values? Acknowledge moments of conflict where your values were tested. How did you respond, and what did you learn?

Am I living in alignment with my values? This is perhaps the most crucial question. If you find discrepancies between your values and your actions, it may be time to revise your commitments.

By revisiting these questions, you can identify the values that resonate with your true self and revise any areas where you've compromised your authenticity for the sake of conformity or acceptance.

"Embracing Change"

The act of revision is inherently tied to the acceptance of change. Change is an inevitable part of life, yet it often brings discomfort. When we seek to align our lives with our true selves, we may have to confront relationships, habits, and environments that no longer serve us. This can be particularly challenging, as loyalty and attachment can complicate our ability to let go.

To navigate this process, consider the following steps:

Acknowledge your feelings. Allow yourself to feel the weight of potential loss—whether it's letting go of a friendship that has become toxic or shifting away from a career path that doesn't fulfill you.

Visualize your future self. What does your life look like when you live in alignment with your values? Creating a mental image can help you clarify what you need to release and what to embrace.

Take small steps. Change doesn't have to be abrupt. Start with small revisions—alter a routine, engage in new activities, or introduce yourself to new people who align with your aspirations.

The Art of Letting Go. Letting go is an art that requires courage and resilience. It is about relinquishing the familiar in favor of the authentic. In his book The Gifts of Imperfection, Brené Brown emphasizes the importance of letting go of what no longer serves us as a way to cultivate authenticity. Brown's insights highlight that the path to a fulfilling life often necessitates the shedding of expectations—both from ourselves and from others.

Letting go can manifest in various ways: it might involve ending a friendship, changing jobs, or even redefining how we perceive ourselves. Each act of release is a step toward clarity. Embrace the discomfort that comes with change; it signifies growth and a commitment to living authentically.

"Cultivating a Supportive Environment"

As you engage in reflection and revision, consider the influence of your environment. Surround yourself with individuals who uplift and inspire you. Community plays a pivotal role in sustaining your commitment to authenticity. Engaging with like-minded individual scan provide support, encouragement, and accountability.

Creating a supportive environment also means setting boundaries with those who drain your energy or undermine your self-worth. As you establish these boundaries, remind yourself that prioritizing your well-being is not selfish—it is a necessary act of self-love.

"Continuous Growth"

Finally, understand that reflection and revision are not one-time acts; they are ongoing processes. Life is dynamic, and our understanding of ourselves evolves with each experience. Embrace the idea that growth is a journey rather than a destination. Regularly carve out time for reflection, allowing yourself the grace to adapt and revise as needed.

In a world that often values speed and surface-level interactions, committing to reflection and revision can set you apart. It is an invitation to deepen your understanding of yourself and cultivate a life that resonates with your true essence.

As you close this chapter, consider your own reflections. What revisions are you ready to make? What commitments will you uphold, and what will you release? The answers to these questions are not only revealing; they are transformative. Your journey of authenticity awaits—take that first step with courage and intention.

Acknowledgments

First and foremost, I want to give thanks to the Most High for making every blessing in my life possible. I never take any of it for granted, and I am truly humbled by the path I've been allowed to walk. To my kids—Rihanna, Robert Jr., Jaylen, and Michael—you are my motivation every single day. You keep me pushing forward, always striving to be the best version of myself. I love you more than words can express, and everything I do is with you in mind.

To my sisters—Monique, Danielle, Nita, and Lynette—I love you all more than you'll ever know. Your support has always been a constant in my life, and I carry that love with me wherever I go.

To my friends—Coka, Cade, Jnan, Prom, Foe, Swole, Scott, Loveha, Kirk, Don, Adam, Cord, Varney, Freak, Cam, Poncho, Sm, George, Tae, Eli, Kennetik, Flamo, Wayne, John Lam and so many others who've shown real love—you are my family, and I'm grateful for each of you. You motivate me just as much as I motivate you. I know we're all going to see our dreams unfold, and I can't wait to share that success with you.

A special thanks to Durk. When you signed me back in 2015, it was more than a business move—it was validation that my talents mattered. You showed me that being on the front line was worth it, and for that, I'll always be grateful.

To Nick Cannon, thank you for always being there when it mattered most. Your belief in me and your ability to help me execute through the tough times is something I'll forever appreciate.

To Courtney, thank you for keeping me on my toes and always being a solid presence in my life. Your support never goes unnoticed, and I value everything you've done for me.

I want to thank my friend that passed away, Kevin "Moose" Leyani. You were one of the realest friends I ever came across. You helped shape me to write this book on loyalty because you showed me what a real friend was supposed to look like. I'll always and forever miss you, and I know you're watching down, making sure I'm on point! I'm happy I had the chance to be your friend! My brother. Thank you.

Finally, to the city of Chicago—you raised me, turned a boy into a man. Those streets shaped who I am today, and if you can make it out of Chicago, you can make it anywhere. Forever legend, forever grateful.

Thank you to everyone who has been part of this journey. We're just getting started.

With all my love and respect,

Robert "Hypno Carlito" Amparan

Made in the USA
Monee, IL
21 May 2025

17869060R00062